How bei STUBBORN, depressed, & UNPOPULAR Saved My Life.

by Jenipher Lyn

ISBN: 978-0-9915651-0-8

2013 first edition

www.jenipherlyn.com
www.doodledream.com
Jenipherlyn@gmail.com

Camilo,
I never thought I'd find someone who would love
and embrace me BECAUSE of my uniqueness. Thanks
for loving me, talking like muppets with me, and
being there for me always. I love you so so much
more than donuts. <3

being "ALONE" IS THE NEW "HAVING FRIENDS"

Friends. Or... No Friends. Yet.

One of my BIGGEST goals in life is to try my BEST to ensure young women grow up feeling secure and LOVED.

Life can be such a LONELY, sad, SCARY world when you don't feel supported physically and emotionally! I've been there, and hated it! Although it's horrible and exhausting... it's truly helped me become the person i am now, and you know what? I really like THIS GIRL! Hooray! About TIME!

This book is the outcome of love, TEARS, depression, & surviving an eating disorder.

It's a compilation of ALL of the things I WISHED more people told me!!!

Sometimes i FREAK OUT that "life is short" and I WASTED so much of it being sad.

-it makes me anxious-

Dear 14 year old me,

I'm so freaking PROUD OF YOU, lady! You stayed true to YOU all these years!! You somehow ignored EVERYONE who pressured you, made fun of you... You don't wish you were a boy anymore, in FACT you love that you are a girl! You're not being told your sensitivity is a weakness -- because it's NOT. AND you're strong enough that if someone does tell you that you know it's THEIR ignorance. You've gone through a LOT of ups and downs and it's been very hard and although life still throws curve balls, you're better equipted to handle it. You like being short now. And having freckles! Oh, And your arms are NOT hairy. NOT AT ALL! It's a SHAME you wore that UGLY sweater for almost 365 days in 6th grade. Even in Summer... EWWW.

All and All, things are MUCH better now. It took time, and LOTS of persistance, but HOORAY! You even have a LOT of friends that care a TON about you!! Who would have thought?

love ♥,
- JENNNN
age 29, married to BOY, living in NYC

hmm... who knew i would be sooo thank-full i was UN popular.

[IN SCHOOL]

I went to a prep school where 90% were 'popular' and the other 10% were not... in the lunch room there was ONE, just one table for us unpopular folk at the end of the cafeteria near the exit..

While talking to a friend the other day about our lives during middle school together, i realized how THANKFUL i am that i was UNPOPULAR. Because of my 'status', i missed out on a lot of the 'normal kid' pressures more often than my popular peers.

I never got asked out, which at the time made me sad, but meant i wasn't pressured for sex. And wasn't invited to very many parties, which means i wasn't often pressured to drink or to try other substances. I realize THIS wont be the norm for everyone, not even close... but at 8, 10, 15 even, i never realize how glad i would be for my unpopularity.

Yesterday, while waiting for the NYC metro, 2 girls in their early 20's were discussing how many guys they've been intimiate with, the frat they were going to that night, and how far they'd go with a guy...

("depends on how drunk they are.")

Then they discussed how LAME one of their cousins is because she's "19 and doesn't party"; "Poor her" they said, because she hasn't kissed a guy yet. My heart hurt for the cousin, and how she was being looked down on for being true to herself, even when she's been made fun of once or twice, and maybe even pressured as well.

I stood there dumbfounded and cringing over their last remark. They were TECHNICALLY making fun of ME. I was 19 before i had MY first kiss, and you know what? Before that I wasn't ready!! I never went to parties either. And i find nothing wrong with that! If you'd rather read books, than read books, and if you actually DO like to party, go for it! Just stick to what YOU like to do, and don't let others bully you!

I can't tell the 19 year old cousin, but i can tell YOU. Stand by what you believe in, NO MATTER WHAT. And stand up for yourself! Trusting yourself is one of the MOST important things you can learn, and I will cheer on EACH and EVERY one of you to learn it early!

tell everyone to SHUT -UP- you are GREAT just the way you are!

this was the day katie told me it was awesome that i was waiting till marriage to have sex.

(even my parents thought i was INSANE)

Have you ever felt unlovable? A feeling so incredibly heartbreaking, yet so many people young and old feel it. Including myself. :(

BUT there is HOPE. Once we learn how to accept ourselves. Really really accept ourselves [which will come with age! I PROMISE!!!] it does get better!

i Feel like an outsider often.

-and just generally feel like folks dont .like. me... even though i know it's false-

As someone who never felt like I belonged, i feel ya sister!! As icky as it sounds, i have to constantly REMIND MYSELF I'm loved, and even liked! Even moments after I'm told

You are SO freaking loveable! Even when you don't feel like i You ARE!!!

 This is VERY important to remember.

BUT what can we do when people DON'T like us? Sometimes you meet someone and you just CLICK... And sometimes you meet someone and you don't get along at all.

Don't be hard on yourself about these times!! It happens. No everyone is going to like you, just like you're not going to like everyone. You're not here to make friends with the WHOLE world. And when you meet the friends you really clic with... it won't matter as much who you don't really get along with.

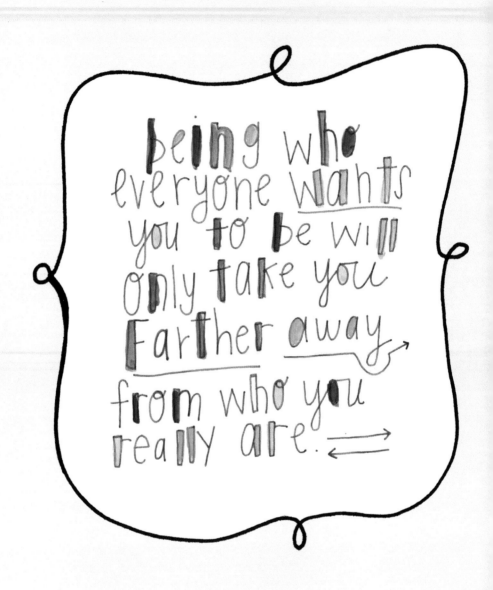

being who everyone wants you to be will only take you Farther away, from who you really are.

Self Love. It's SO important

If i look back to my past, i had so much confidence! When i was 6, i wasn't afraid of talking to people, or asking for things... of saying what i wanted... but somehow along the way, those brave feelings left. :(

i wish confidence would introduce itself to me...

i would be so thrilled..!

While watching a movie the other day, the main character said something that rubbed me the wrong way. She said "Psh, guys don't like smart girls." I was FURIOUS! What a bunch of BOLOGNA! Immediately, I started writing a page for this book!

Ironically, moments after i started writing this, the main char-cter met a boy who liked smart girls, so she started studying to impress him. I calmed down about the "Smart Girls" comment, but it brought me to a completely different topic:

Ge yourself

When you are being YOURSELF, the right people will be {d r a w n} to you. Having people really GET you, even just ONE person, is really important. Whether it's a family member or a friend, having that person who understands you will bring you such JOY and will help you feel less alone.

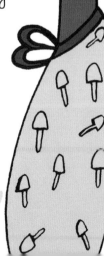

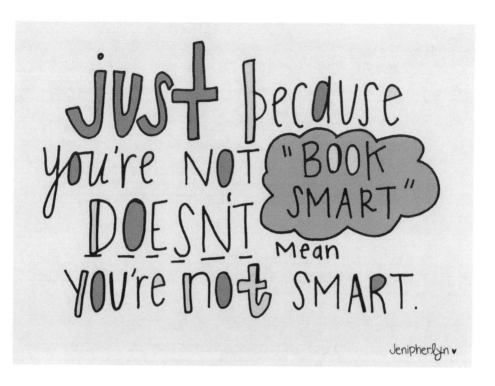

just because you're NOT "BOOK SMART" DOESN'T mean you're not SMART.

Jenipherlyn ♥

"HOLY CRAP!!! I'm NOT DUMB!!!"
It wasn't until i was 26, and working at an awful cubicle job that i had this realization.

I jumped up from my seat in my cubicle, and ran to hug my friend who sat beside me. It was [sadly] the first time in my ENTIRE LIFE and i learned that i wasn't stupid, and i was THRILLED.

...in third grade i took a scantron test that determined how smart i was' for my ENTIRE school career. Sadly for me, and my ADD tendencies, i christmas tree'd it, and was shoved into the 'stupid people classes' until i left the school when i was a junior in highschool.

19

As an adult, I FINALLY understand that there are so many differernt KINDS of smart-ness!!
Some people are book-smart, some street-smart, or business-savvy.. some might even be a smart-A [har har!!

But let me be the first to tell you...
You are NOT DUMB!!!!!!

Some people are "right-brained": creative, artistic, an open-minded thinker who perceives things in subjective terms. Or perhaps you're more of a "left-brained" person, where you're analytical, good at tasks that require attention to detail, and more logically minded.

Many of us specialize in certain things. Some people are smart in finances, while others are great artists. ALL of us understand certain subjects but not others. And that's okay!

Let people LOVE you.

"I have trouble "burdening" others when i'm feeling sad, so i end up sitting by myself playing the evil voices over and over."

you're a burden. you're a burden.
No one cares. Debby Downer.

I hope you NEVER hear these evil voices... it's one of the MOST difficult things i've gone against. [and BOY life is hard sometimes]

I'll let you in on a hidden secret!
People DO care about you; even if it doesn't always feel that way! And these people WANT to help you when you're feeling awful! Believe me... whenever I finally share what I've been feeling with someone i trust, I feel SO much better! And I end up feeling lighter and less alone. Yay!!

^ magazine ^

Pretend-ing Not to like something is SO draining

22

I remember the days when i invited my "friends" over, and RUSHED home from school on a MISSION!!

Operation: Get-Rid-Of-Everything-That-Will-Help-Them-Make-Fun-Of-Me.

I got really good at it too, hiding posters of cute boys behind calendars, and moving cds and movies to closets. And somehow... i'd always miss one! So annoying! It took SO MUCH energy to hide things that i loved, that soon enough, i just stopped inviting people over period.

Sometimes it's MUCH easier to be alone, than to be with crappy friends.

Chapter 3

Depression freaking SUCKS

i FEEL...
forgettable

The sound of white noise was faintly playing in the background when I fell asleep after the 8th... okay fine, the 10th movie I watched in my room. When i was 18, the local librarians might not of known me by name, but they knew me by height... height of the 20 VHS tapes I borrowed each time... [This was before DVDs kids!! we used bulky VHS tapes] Did I mention I would watch all 20 of these in a row, by myself??

nerdy

indie

romance

When you're depressed, you don't often want to see ANYONE. Like, ever... But at the same time, you're sooo lonely you could cry... wishing someone would see you behind your angry exterior, and literally FIGHT YOU to hug you. That someone would stay even if your words are vile... even though, you wouldn't stay yourself. So why would someone else stay?

It's the most BIZARRE, CRAZY, CONFUSING, ANGRY, LONELY feeling in the world... and if i'm honest, i still deal with these demons. But not QUITE in the same way. Thank GOD!!!

"Why Bother? I'm gonna die anyways..." I thought while laying on my bed, staring at the ceiling, one afternoon.

I was 18, and it was one of the BAD days. One of those days I felt lonley, sad, and like NOTHING mattered. I had had lots of bad days up to that point, but never thought of suicide. This time was one of the few times i actually SCARED myself with my OWN thoughts.

This was the very FIRST time I recall asking for help, like really asking for help. I stuck a note to a book i was reading, "When Nothing Matters Anymore", and put the book in the laundry room, begging my Mom for a counselor.

It's freaking scary asking for help, but GOOD GOLLY, i am SO thankful i did!!

Sometimes taking a Risk is the scariest thing in world... but, really worth it! Really!!

things do matter. It may not feel like it, but they do

you matter

I can't express HOW
IMPORTANT this
statement is.

I hope you BELIEVE IT.

I'll remind you.
Promise.

I sat on the floor in the bathroom crying for the 3rd time since we moved into our new apt... and I'm sure my boyfriend was tired of dealing with me since i can't seem to form words when i'm sad or crying. But love is for ALWAYS. Even during the crappy times!

Sometimes when you're super dooper sad, you don't want someone to help you 'figure it out'; you just want someone to BE THERE while you SOB like a mouse that needs an oil change...what? no one else sounds like a oil-change-needing mouse?

There's something really magical when you find someone [a friend, family member, or significant other] who really understands that!!

sometimes all i need is someone to hold me when i cry.

"I can't tell you THIS because you can't handle it!"

This is a statement i've heard my ENTIRE life and i HATE IT!! It took me YEARS to realize that being sensitive is NOT a bad thing!

i am a... {HSP} Hyper-sensitive person

Being sensitive is NOT NOT NOT a weakness!!
Yes it makes life more difficult. Yes, i cry more often and feel things REALLY deeply.. but being sensitive is the REASON i can empathize with people so much! It's the REASON i LOVE encouraging people! And it's the reason i wanted to write this book!

i wish people didnt view my sensitivity as a bad thing

I don't know when it starts, but WAY too early in life, we start to become REALLY critical of ourselves.

stop being so hard on yourself.

please?

you are
so
much
{STRONGER}
then you
realize.

Chapter 4

STOP
comparing
your self 2
Others

You are AWESOME.
Just the way you are. Seriously!!
I'm not your mom, so you HAVE to believe me!

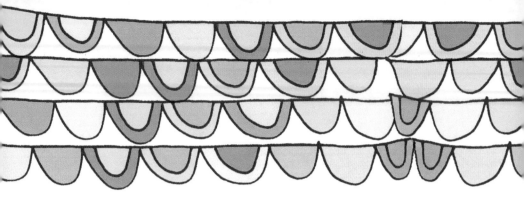

Have you ever **hated** your body?

I know i have!! And really... who hasn't?
I can honestly and truthfully say that
EVERYONE has at one point or another...
and it's such a shame.

We are such lovely creatures... so why
do we feel like we aren't "enough".. ?

Why do we feel like we have to change
ourselves.. to be **beautiful?**

i hate my body...

cookies

It pretty much makes me sick how focused we all are on our weight. Which means I make myself sick!! I've struggled with my eating my whole life, but in 2009 it was by far the WORST I've ever been. In 2009 I had an eating disorder.

My eating disorder was classified as anorexica nervosa.

Anorexia nervosa:
Anorexia nervosa is an eating disorder that makes people lose more weight than is considered healthy for their age and height. Persons with this disorder may have an intense fear of weight gain, even when they are underweight. They may diet or exercise too much or use other ways to lose weight.

And I was the "restricting type" which meant I kept my diet to only a tiny bit of certain foods to make sure I didn't gain any weight. Since I'm a smaller person by nature, i feel people didn't realize how sick I was right away... which was something I was happy about at the time, but that was also really dangerous too.

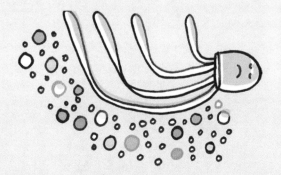

During all of this, God blessed with me with one o
the WORST jobs I've ever had... AND some of the
BEST coworkers I could even pray for. These people
saved me.

"You look like you're from Ethiopia."

This comment, said in complete truth, was the first
time someone told me outright that I was actually
TOO THIN. Too THIN! Can you believe it? Is there ever
such a thing??? What crazies they were! But this
was the statement that changed everything. Because
it came from two boys who didn't love me [and
didn't have a filter, thank God!] After that, I
started seeing a nutritionist that specialized in Eatin
Disorders.

being
thin,
skinny,
... SMALL ...
doesn't make
you =
- beautiful -

you are perfect
the way
you are.

"You look so good!" She said...
"It's because you look so skinny!"

A comment like that, even when meant well, is very dangerous. Immediately when my friend said this to me, in all sincerity, I knew it was a topic I needed to cover. Drastically.

The CURSE of being a naturally small person is that people think it's actually OKAY to comment on your weight. The reason my usual 'weight gains' were "drastic" was because even the slightest change on my super short frame looked extremely apparent.

The last time people gave me oodles of compliments like that was back in 2010. "Omgosh you look so good!" is what they actually said, after years of mentioning weight gains during their 'hellos'. At the time, I appreciated these comments. These people loved me! Whether they realized it or not, this one comment, "omgosh you look so good!" fueled my insanely unhealthy lifestyle, and made feeling terrible all the time easier to deal with.

These people didn't have to know that I had bad headaches all the time, or that I was always cold, even in summer. They didn't have to know that I hadn't been grocery shopping in months... or that my hair was falling out. The only REAL difference in my appearance back then was that, at the time, I was at my lowest weight since middle school. Little did they know I wasn't eating and was actually really sick.

I remember my nutritionist telling me what to eat when i was learning how to eat again. and she said i could have salad, AND a yogurt AND an apple and THEN i could still have dessert if i wanted!!! And i was FLOORED... wow! I was "allowed" to have ALL of that?!?!

 **breakfast**

Two eggs scrambled with munster cheese & 2 pieces of fake bacon sandwiched between a slice of toast i cut in half = EASY egg sandwich! If i'm still hungry i'll have 1/2 an orange & a few slices of apple.

lunch

California sushi rolls. Side salad with Honey dressing. And LOTS of tea!!!

Dinner

A bowl of pasta with veggies, chick'n nuggets & a salad. & i can STILL have dessert!! yay!!

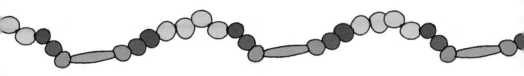

I wish I spent my life EMBRACING my differences. This morning while getting on the subway I heard 3 teenaged girls chatting one said how much she loves being short. I love that!

When I was her age I was constantly!!! upset for not being this... or that... Taller, bigger boobs, whatever... And I wish just Appreciated myself.

i Refuse ② FeeL Guilt or Shame for what My Body LOOKS like

Chapter 5

Following your heart's PASSIONS
makes life GRAND!

I asked a bunch of my friends what they wish they heard more of growing up; "YOU ARE ENOUGH" came up over and over. And it's such a TRUE statement.

It's so hard looking at friends throughout our lives and feeling that we're not as pretty or smart as them... and feeling like we are lacking or don't have the gifts they have. And it takes a LOT of time to realize that we ARE ENOUGH. We are ALL completely different, and it's SUCH a blessing!! How boring would life be if we ALL wanted to be chefs, or jewelry makers or teachers....

i am enough.

YOU have a PURPOSE

We are all COMPLETELY different!
Because we are so different from one another, I am a firm
believer that we ALL have different purposes. And once you
figure out yours, life gets SO MUCH BETTER!!! I promise!

Throughout your life you will try lots of different things;
some activities will stick, some will feel like chores. My
purpose journey took me to jewelry making at age 9, horseback
riding, making doll house food, painting, food photography,
fashion design, and FINALLY illustration. And although i've
been selling my jewelry for over 10 years and selling my
illustrations for three... things didn't "click" until i started
writing this book. (Hooray for this book!)

Keep persistently doing things you love, and eventually you'll
find your purpose too! THEN once you find it, DIG IN and learn
as much as you can. DEVOUR your craft and you'll FLOURISH!

51

it's HARD WORK changing the WORLD... but it's soo WORTh it.

What you do, at any age, is SO important and often keeps you {alive} when life is hard. I don't know where I'd be today without ART. Throughout most of my life, ART continually kept me sane. And for that I'm so thankful!! So whether you love dogs, plants, cooking, writing, magic, politics, painting, inventing things, or even health, DREAM DREAM DREAM!! Watch videos that inspire you! Do things that make you EXCITED. Don't worry if other people don't think your passion matters or if it's cool. JUST DO IT!!

Ask your parents [nicely ;)] to take you to events related to you passion; like art shows, or museums...

The W⊕rld Needs YOU!

Whether you feel like it or not, we were given different gifts for a reason. Each person has a different purpose in this life, and if you already know what you LOVE and what you feel passionate about.... GO FOR IT!!!

just do it.
there's no right or wrong.

at age 15:

Mom, can I get these Sesame street plates?

NO.

at age 21:

MOM, can I get these sesame street bandaids?

NO, your too old for sesame street!

at age 29:

MOM can i have these sesame street pancake molds?

sure! I know ya love sesame street! - mom

i wish
some one
EXplaINEd
to me that
It's so
important
to try...
and
fail.

EVERY LITTLE BIT COUNTS.

It didn't seem like it helped in the moment but EVERY single time i started a food drive, tried to get a recycling program at work or at school, and EVEN when my best friend Amanda and picked up ciggerete butts when we were 6. It ALL makes a difference!

Sometimes it doesn't feel like its making a difference, but try to ignore these feelings! If your heart's in the right place, they ALL MATTER. Things may not end up the way you hoped but you NEVER know who will be inspired by you, or what THEY might start after watching what you've tried to do!

I even got 200 signatures for the recycling program [like they asked for!] before they told me they "just dont want to have recycling." But that's NOT going to STOP me from trying again one day if i find another place that needs to learn about the wonderful world of recycling!!

we all have different gifts and talents, but we are all equal.

Hey kids, ^ ^ these are called cassette tapes

today i will {try to} be thankful.

Gratitude: even just one thing each day will make life {feel} BETTER!

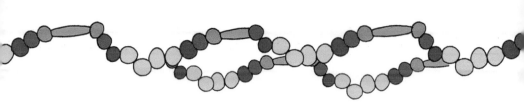

She was thank-FULL
she made it
through all
those
hard
times.

You might be going through A LOT right now... but lets chat quickly about what you're thankful for right now. There is always at least ONE THING. It could be supertiny... but it ALL counts! Here... i'll help you get started!!

Thankful LIST!!!

drawing Betsy 🐛 comics

green tea w/ milk

hi

Dear YOU.

YOU. ARE. AWESOME.

I'm super proud of you for just BEING YOU. That's one of the hardest things you can do, and you're DOING IT! [or at least trying to, which counts!!]

Right now i bet all of your feelings feel CRAZY, BIG, REAL, and HARD to deal with. And they are. But i promise you'll look back in 3, 6, 15 months, and some of these feelings might have dissolved already: new feelings in their place. And on those hardest of hard days, i have faith you'll be able to PUSH THROUGH. There is a GIANT unicorn-sized light in the MIDDLE of the tunnel to look forward to. And it's CLOSER than you think!
Really! It is!!

Sending hugs, rainbows, and chocolate chip cookie vibes your way!

-Jenipher

PS: Let me know how you're doing! My inbox is always open!!
Jenipherlyn@gmail.com

holy moly! thank you!!!

HOLY MOLY, I am SO grateful for EVERYONE who helped me plan, and prep, and INSPIRED ME!! there are SO many people to thank!!!!

♥ ♥

CAMILO!!	Roe O	Katie A	Beth
Mi Famila!!	Laura P.	Veronica M	Jeanne
Brandy W	Khara D,	Julissa M	Margaret S.
Jenny Lecter	Georgia C.	Michelle W	Margot Z
Lindsey W	Lisa G	Amanda G	Tamara R
Alyssa A	Sheila D	Yolli S	Melody R
Jacqui B.	Jessie S	Bethany	Lauren F.
Carolyn L.	Carissa	Tiffany B	June B.
Jenny Lipper	Dan Lugo	Kelsey C.	Torin D.

Caitie S, Thank you for all of your time, suggestions, and honesty. My book is now a ZILLION times better because of YOU! <3

Friends, thank you for believing in me, for inspiring me, for teaching me i HAVE a VOICE, and just letting me babble when i needed to!

And good GOLLY, thank you to ALLLLL of my INCREDIBLE Kickstarter supporters. This is coming true because of YOUR help!! YAY!!!

P.S YOU MATTER!!

YEP!

Books, films, and websites that will SURELY inspire!

This is a list compiled by myself, and my helpful friends. Please make sure it's approprite for you [or your child's] age bracket. I'll have a list of even MORE suggestions on my website too! These are just some i really think are wonderful [or sounded amazing!]

* "Indie Kindred" a film by Jen Lee
* "Pippi Longstockings" - i love this movie!
* "When Nothing Matters Anymore" by Bev Cobain
* "Page by Paige" by Laura Lee Gulledge
* "Hyperbowl and a Half" by Allie Brosh
* "How to be Alone" a film by Andrea Dorfman

Great websites!

www.rookie.com
www.bravegirlsclub.com
www.twloha.com
www.hellogiggles.com

Specific for Eating Disorder:
* Neda.com
* Geneen Roth
* "Living Without Ed" by Jenni Schaefer
* Please let me know if you'd like the name of my nutirtionist in Florida

If you are in crisis or thinking about hurting yourself, call the National Suicide Lifeline at 1-800-273-8255 to speak immediately to a free, trained counselor.

Also! A national 24-hour, toll free confidential suicide hotline for gay and questioning youth. www.thetrevorproject.org/